Pairs Trading: A Bayesian Example

Stefan Hollos and J. Richard Hollos

Disclaimer

Abrazol Publishing

an imprint of Exstrom Laboratories LLC
662 Nelson Park Drive, Longmont, CO 80503-7674 U.S.A.

Pairs Trading: A Bayesian Example
Stefan Hollos and J. Richard Hollos
ISBN: 978-1-887187-152
Copyright ©2012 by Exstrom Laboratories LLC

About the Cover

Sawtooth Mountain from Cony Flats. This picture was taken on Aug 8, 2009 by Stefan and Richard Hollos. Approximate coordinates: +40.12985, -105.57651.

Contents

1

Introduction

This book shows you how to find relationships between stocks or exchange traded funds (ETFs) using Bayesian analysis. A relationship that most traders are probably familiar with is linear correlation. This is sometimes used as the basis for pairs trading. But linear correlation is just one way that stocks or ETFs can be related. The analysis we will present in this book can be used to exploit almost any kind of relationship that may exist between stocks or ETFs. The book will show how to calculate the probability of a stock or ETF ending the day up or down based on what other stocks or ETFs are doing. A probability is more useful than a simple up or down signal. It quantifies the certainty of a prediction and allows a trader to take a position consistent with a given level of risk. Any active trader should find the techniques presented in this book useful. We are only going to examine the relationships in one small group of ETFs as an example of what is possible but the same techniques will work for any set of stocks, ETFs, or even bonds.

In particular we are going to look at dependencies between the returns on SPY and a handful of other ETFs. SPY is the ticker symbol for an ETF that tracks the price and dividend yield of the S&P 500 Index. The S&P 500 Index is composed of 500 stocks of companies in 24 different industry groups. SPY is therefore a good representative of equities as a general investment class. It is also one of the oldest and most liquid ETFs with daily trading volume in the tens of millions of shares. The fact that SPY is one of the older ETFs means that there is a significant amount of historical data available which we will need in the analysis.

The other ETFs (11 of them) were chosen to represent bonds, commodities, currencies, and other equities. All the ETF's chosen have daily data going back to at least the start of 2007. This gives us sufficient data for experimenting. We will use the data to find statistical relationships between the returns on these ETFs and the returns on SPY that we can use for statistical arbitrage trading. The type of arbitrage we are talking about is similar to pairs trading, one of the oldest forms of statistical arbitrage. The general idea is to use the returns on these ETFs to calculate the probability that

SPY will end the day with a positive or negative return. When the trend is against the most probable outcome it may be the signal for a possible trading opportunity.

The other ETFs used in the analysis are as follows:

TLT - Barclays 20+ Year Treasury Bond Fund. The fund invests in US treasury bonds with a long term maturity of 20 years or more.
http://us.ishares.com/product_info/fund/overview/TLT.htm

IEF - Barclays 7-10 Year Treasury Bond Fund. The fund invests in US treasury bonds with an intermediate maturity of 7 to 10 years.
http://us.ishares.com/product_info/fund/overview/IEF.htm

SHY - Barclays 1-3 Year Treasury Bond Fund. The fund invests in US treasury bonds with a short term maturity of 1 to 3 years.
http://us.ishares.com/product_info/fund/overview/SHY.htm

QQQ - PowerShares QQQ. The fund invests in all of stocks in the NASDAQ 100 Index. These are 100 of the largest domestic and international nonfinancial companies listed on the Nasdaq.
http://www.invescopowershares.com/products/overview.aspx?ticker

XLF - Financial Select Sector SPDR. Tracks the S&P Financial Select Sector Index (IXM).
https://www.spdrs.com/product/fund.seam?ticker=XLF

LQD - iBoxx Investment Grade Corporate Bond Fund.

Tracks the corporate bond market represented by the iBoxx Liquid Investment Grade Index.
http://us.ishares.com/product_info/fund/overview/LQD.htm

GLD - SPDR Gold Shares. Tracks the price of gold bullion. Backed by physical possession of gold.
http://www.spdrgoldshares.com/

USO - United States Oil Fund. Tracks west Texas intermediate light sweet crude oil.
http://www.unitedstatesoilfund.com/

EWZ - MSCI Brazil Index Fund. Tracks the Brazilian stock market represented by the MSCI Brazil Index.
http://us.ishares.com/product_info/fund/overview/EWZ.htm

FXC - CurrencyShares Canadian Dollar Trust. Tracks the price of the Canadian Dollar in terms of U.S. Dollars.
http://www.currencyshares.com/products/overview.rails?symbol=FXC

FXE - CurrencyShares Euro Trust. Tracks the price of the Euro in terms of U.S. Dollars.
http://www.currencyshares.com/products/overview.rails?symbol=FXE

We will start by looking at how well the individual daily open to close returns of each of these ETFs predicts the performance of SPY for that day. For example suppose we know that TLT was up 0.5% for the day, then what does that tell us about the probability that SPY ended the day with a positive or negative return.

Next we will look at how well the returns from groups of ETFs of size 2, 3, and 4 predict the return on SPY. Once again suppose that TLT was up 0.5% for the day but now we also know that QQQ was down 0.25%. Does this new piece of information improve the ability to correctly say if SPY ended up or down? It turns out that adding more information generally does improve things but not always.

The tool we use to calculate the probability of a positive or negative return on SPY is called a Bayesian classifier. It is called a classifier because it calculates probabilities for only two discrete outcomes: positive or negative. Let A be the event where SPY closes positive (close is above the open) and let B be the event where it closes negative (close is below the open). The goal is to calculate the probabilities of A and B given information about the return on one of the other ETFs. These are called conditional probabilities and they are written as $P(A|X)$ and $P(B|X)$, where X is the return on one of the other ETFs. The method we will use to calculate these probabilities is called Bayes' Theorem. This theorem allows us to relate probabilities as follows:

$$P(A|X) = \frac{P(X|A)P(A)}{P(X|A)P(A) + P(X|B)P(B)} \quad (1.1)$$

$$P(B|X) = 1 - P(A|X) \quad (1.2)$$

So to do the calculation we need the probabilities of X given A, X given B, and the unconditional probabilities of A and B. In the language of Bayesian statistics $P(A)$ and $P(B)$ are called the prior probabilities of A and B and we will estimate them using historical data. The estimates will simply be the fraction of times that SPY closed up and down in the historical data. The $P(X|A)$ and $P(X|B)$ probabilities are called likelihood functions and are also estimated using historical data. We will model these as continuous probabililty distributions since the return X can take on a continuous range of values.

There are two ways to estimate such a continuous distribution. One way is to use a parametric approach where we assume that X has a particular distribution such as a Gaussian for example. We then use the historical data to estimate the parameters of the distribution which for a Gaussian would be the mean and standard deviation.

The other way to model a continuous distribution is to be more agnostic and use a nonparametric method called kernel density estimation (KDE) to evaluate the distribution. We are not going to go into exactly how KDE works. You can find explanations for KDE in any book that deals with nonparametric statistics. In essence it allows the data itself to dictate the form of the distribution instead of imposing a preconcieved notion of what the distribution should be. This is important since there is some controversy as to what kind of distribution that returns in the stock market have. There is good evidence that indicates returns are not Gaussian, so trying to impose a Gaussian is probably not a good idea.

In any case, all of the calculations are done by a program called class2kde which is written in the C programming language. The program can be downloaded from our data mining and machine learning web page at:

http://www.exstrom.com/dmml/dmml.html

class2kde is a general purpose program that can be used to explore how well a binary classifier will work on any given data set. The program takes a training file and a class file as input. Each record in the training file is classified using all the other records. The class file is used to check the classifications. The output for each record is the class 1 probability (the probability that the class equals 1) and the true class for the record. This is useful for determining if the features in the training file really are effective in classifying the records.

To create a binary classifier you need training data. Each line in the training data file represents an instance of what it is you are trying to classify. These instances are called records. Each record consists of a set of numbers separated by spaces. The numbers are values of features or attributes of the record. The same number of values must appear on each line. The training data must also have a class file associated with it. Each line in the class file specifies the class of the corresponding record in the training file.

Now exactly how can this information be used for trading? The idea is that once we have found a strong statistical relationship between the price of SPY and some of these other ETFs then we can monitor that relationship during the trading day and bet in a way that assumes it will continue to hold. This will be discussed in more detail below.

2

Preparing the Data

There are two data files we need to create in order to use the program class2kde: the training file and the class file.

Let's start with the class file since it's simpler. We want to do a binary classification of SPY, so the class file will consist of a single column of 0's and 1's, representing for each day (open-to-close) whether SPY went up (1) or down (0). Staying the same is considered down. On our *data mining and machine learning page* is an awk script [1] called `get_stock_ocbinary.awk` for converting the Yahoo Finance CSV data for a ticker to this single column of 0's and 1's. For our example in this book, the

---

[1]awk is available for most operating systems. See the *awk Wikipedia page* for a list of implementations.

class file has 1,388 lines of 0's and 1's, corresponding to SPY's open-to-close over the 1,388 trading days from January 3, 2007 to July 5, 2012.

The training file consists of as many columns of numbers as there are predictors. The columns are separated by a space. We will start by trying to predict SPY with just a single column of numbers, being the fractional change of the open-to-close of another ETF. The fractional change is (close - open)/open. We use this instead of just the price difference (close - open) so there is no drift in the mean. This allows us to be more accurate in evaluating the distribution of the predictor data using kernel density estimation (more on this in the next chapter). We will later add one column at a time to see if multiple ETFs improve the predictability of SPY. Our *data mining and machine learning page* has an awk script called `get_stock_oc.awk` for converting the Yahoo Finance CSV data for a ticker to the fractional change of the open-to-close. For the training file examples in this book, there are 1,388 lines of floating point (decimal) numbers where each number on a line corresponds to the fractional change in the open-to-close of a predictor. The time span for these files is 1,388 trading days from Jan 3, 2007 to July 5, 2012.

There is also a small parameter file (h values) that needs to be created for running class2kde which will be discussed in chapter 4.

3

Visually Identifying the Classification Power of the Data

How do we know whether a chosen predictor whose data has been put in the training file is actually useful for classifying? One way to find out is just run the program class2kde on it and see how well the classification works. Another way to do it, a visual way, is to split the training data into 2 sets. One set has all the training data for those days the class file contains a 0 (0 response). The other set has all the training data for those days the class file contains a 1 (1 response). Then, on a single graph, we plot 2 conditional probability density functions. One for the case where the

11

response is 0, the other for the case where the response
is 1. If the 2 plots have any non-overlapping areas,
then we know the chosen predictor actually has some
predictive power. In this case, we say the predictor has
the ability to classify the predictee.

Figure 3.1 shows the conditional probability density
functions for the return (fractional difference of open-
to-close) on TLT, with lighter for the case where SPY
closes up, and darker for SPY closes down.

The gnuplot command [1] to generate this plot is:

```
plot 'tltoc_r0.dat' using 1:(1./659.) smooth kdensity,
'tltoc_r1.dat' using 1:(1./729.) smooth kdensity
```

where the command is all on one line, and `tltoc_r0.dat`
is the file containing the 0 response data, and `tltoc_r1.dat`
contains the 1 response data. The numbers 659 and 729
are the number of records (lines) in the files `tltoc_r0.dat`
and `tltoc_r1.dat` respectively. Note that the sum of
these 2 numbers, $659 + 729 = 1,388$, is the total number of records in the training file.

In figure 3.1 we can see significant areas of non-overlap.
The darker density function (0 response) is shifted to
the right, and the lighter (1 response) is shifted to the
left. The lighter is also taller than the darker. From
this we can say that the returns on TLT have some

---

[1] *gnuplot* is available for most operating systems.

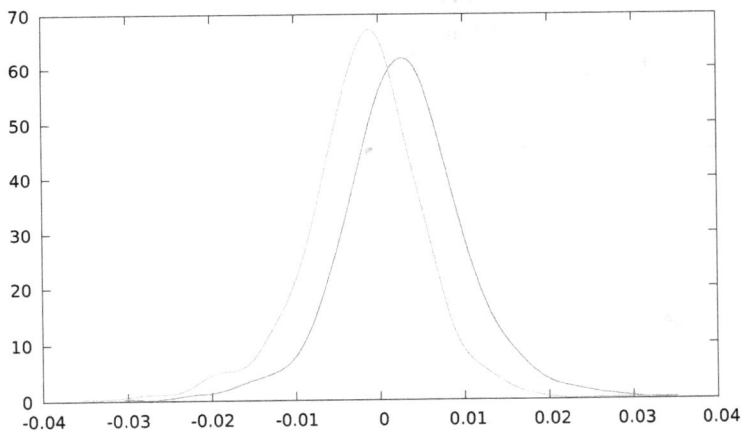

Figure 3.1: Conditional probability density functions for the return on TLT. The lighter is for the case where SPY closes up, and the darker is for the case where it closes down. The density functions are kernel density estimates.

predictive power on whether SPY closes up or down
(open-to-close) for the day. To quantify this, we will
run class2kde in the next chapter.

Similar conditional probability functions for the other
10 predictor ETFs (IEF SHY QQQ XLF LQD GLD
USO EWZ FXC FXE) are shown in figures 3.2 through
3.11. You can see that some of these ETFs are better at
classifying SPY than others. For example TLT, QQQ,
XLF, and EWZ are good classifiers, while GLD and
LQD are poor.

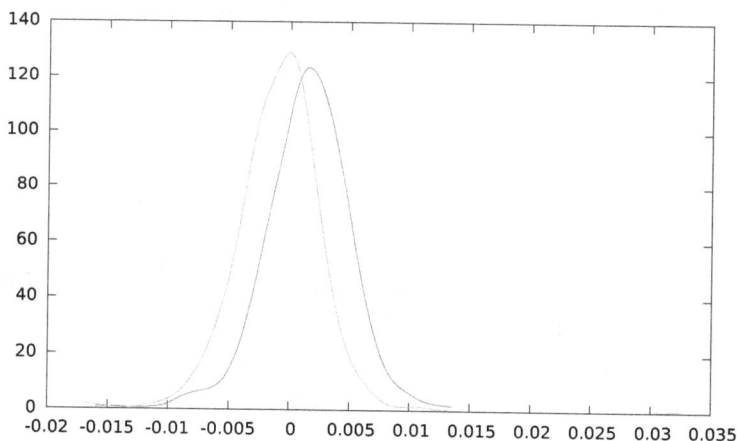

Figure 3.2: Conditional probability density functions
for the return on IEF. The lighter is for the case where
SPY closes up, and the darker is for the case where it
closes down. The density functions are kernel density
estimates.

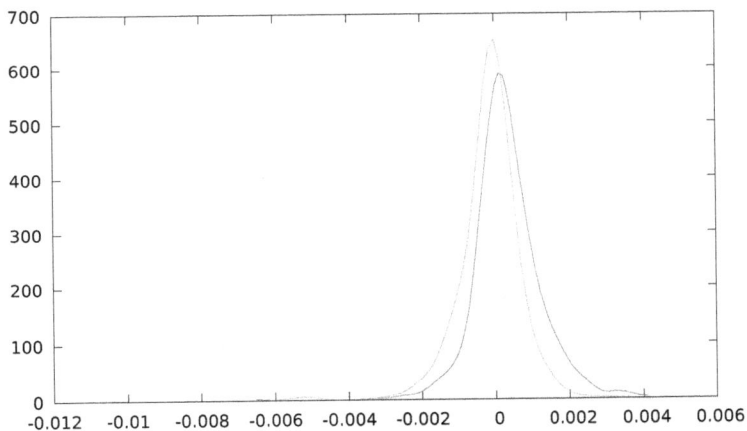

Figure 3.3: Conditional probability density functions for the return on SHY. The lighter is for the case where SPY closes up, and the darker is for the case where it closes down. The density functions are kernel density estimates.

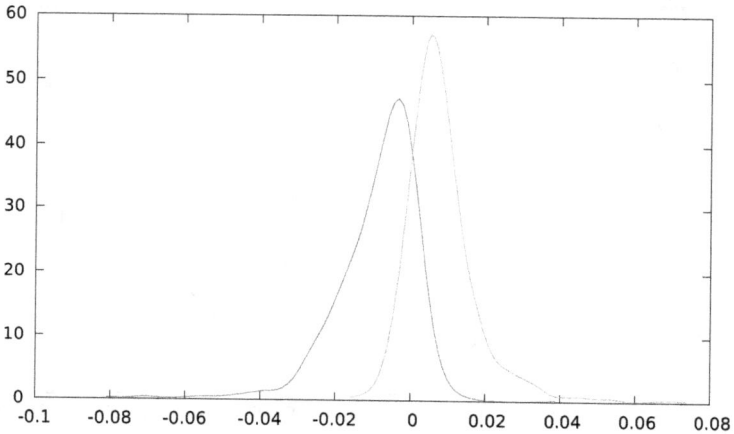

Figure 3.4: Conditional probability density functions for the return on QQQ. The lighter is for the case where SPY closes up, and the darker is for the case where it closes down. The density functions are kernel density estimates.

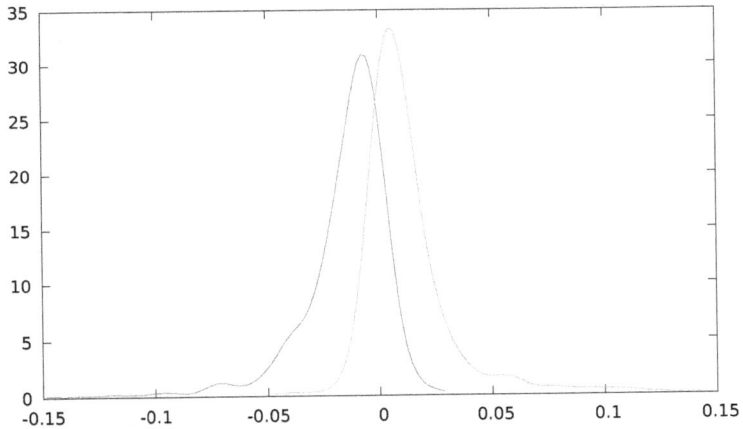

Figure 3.5: Conditional probability density functions for the return on XLF. The lighter is for the case where SPY closes up, and the darker is for the case where it closes down. The density functions are kernel density estimates.

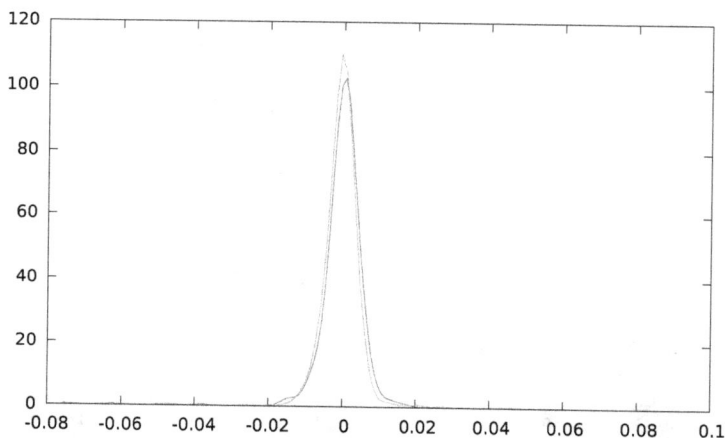

Figure 3.6: Conditional probability density functions
for the return on LQD. The lighter is for the case where
SPY closes up, and the darker is for the case where it
closes down. The density functions are kernel density
estimates.

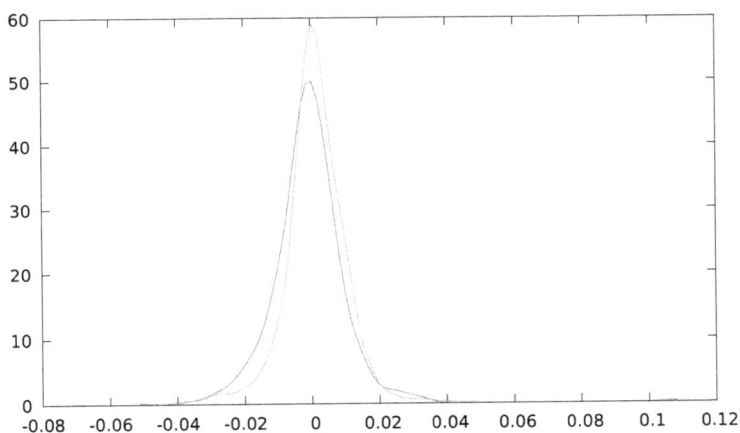

Figure 3.7: Conditional probability density functions for the return on GLD. The lighter is for the case where SPY closes up, and the darker is for the case where it closes down. The density functions are kernel density estimates.

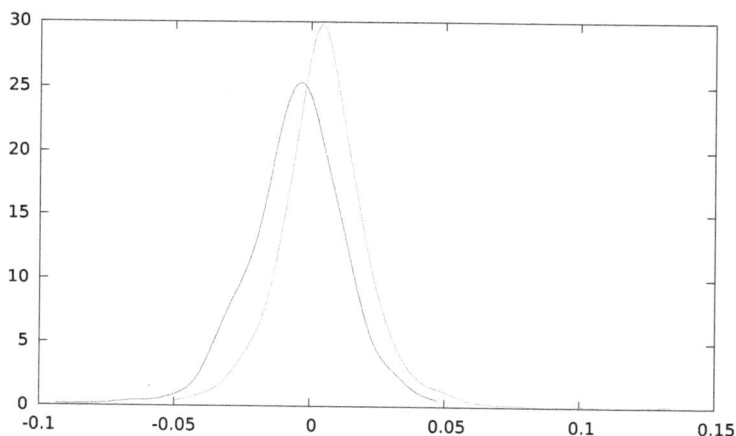

Figure 3.8: Conditional probability density functions for the return on USO. The lighter is for the case where SPY closes up, and the darker is for the case where it closes down. The density functions are kernel density estimates.

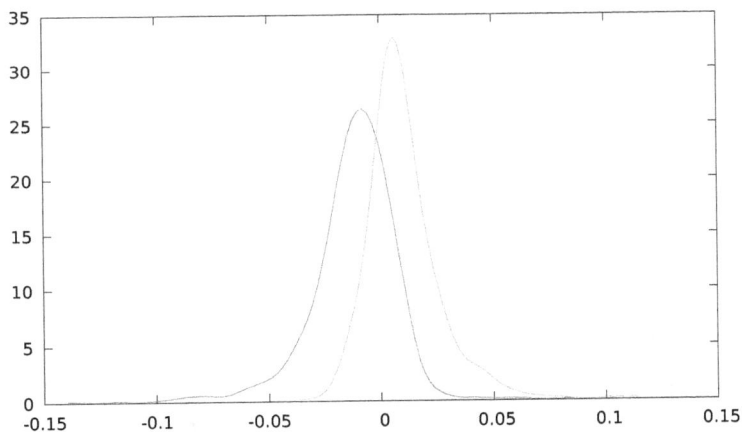

Figure 3.9: Conditional probability density functions for the return on EWZ. The lighter is for the case where SPY closes up, and the darker is for the case where it closes down. The density functions are kernel density estimates.

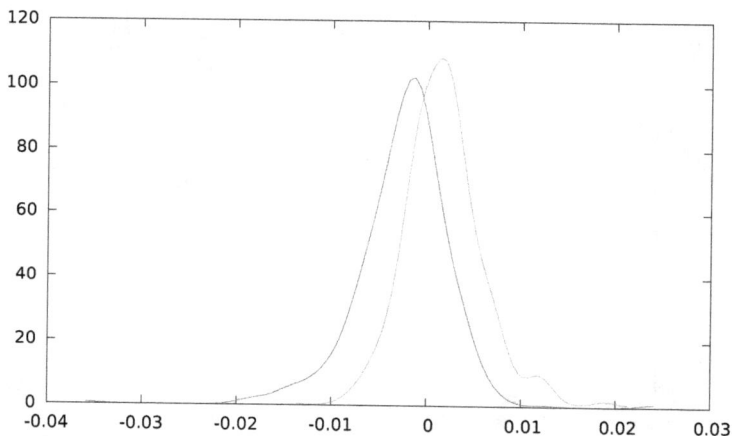

Figure 3.10: Conditional probability density functions
for the return on FXC. The lighter is for the case where
SPY closes up, and the darker is for the case where it
closes down. The density functions are kernel density
estimates.

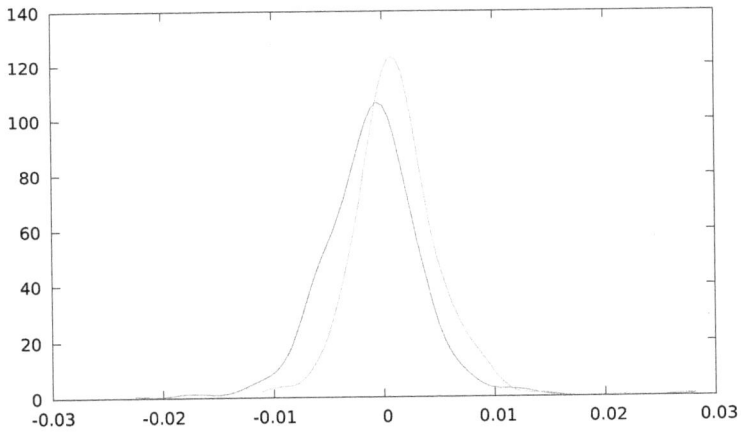

Figure 3.11: Conditional probability density functions for the return on FXE. The lighter is for the case where SPY closes up, and the darker is for the case where it closes down. The density functions are kernel density estimates.

3. VISUALLY IDENTIFYING THE CLASSIFICATION POWER OF THE DATA

4

Running class2kde

In the previous chapter we showed visually the ability of each of 11 ETFs to classify SPY. In this chapter we introduce the class2kde program, describing how its output can be used to classify, and how to use it to produce an ROC curve. We use each of the 11 ETFs to classify SPY, and then see if we can boost the classification power by using more than 1 ETF to classify SPY.

4.1 From output probability to binary classification

Each line of the output of class2kde contains a probability (floating point number between 0 and 1) and the actual result of what happened with SPY for that corresponding day (1 for up, 0 for down or unchanged). For our example with SPY, the 1st line corresponds to Jan 3, 2007, and the last line to July 5, 2012.

The probability is the predicted probability that SPY ended the day up, i.e. that the class was 1. To turn this into an actual prediction, you have to interpret the probabilities by setting a threshold above which the predicted classification will be 1, and below which the predicted classification will be 0. The obvious choice is to use $p > 0.5$ to predict class 1, but this may not always be the optimal choice. You could be more conservative, for example, and use $p > 0.7$ to predict class 1. To analyze this in more detail, we need to look at the 4 possible outcomes of a binary classification.

TP: A True Positive is where the classifier correctly indicates a positive response.

FP: In a False Positive the classifier indicates a positive response where the actual is negative.

TN: A True Negative is where the classifier correctly indicates a negative response.

FN: In a False Negative the classifier indicates a negative response where the actual is positive.

The four results can be organized into what is called a confusion matrix as shown in figure 4.1.

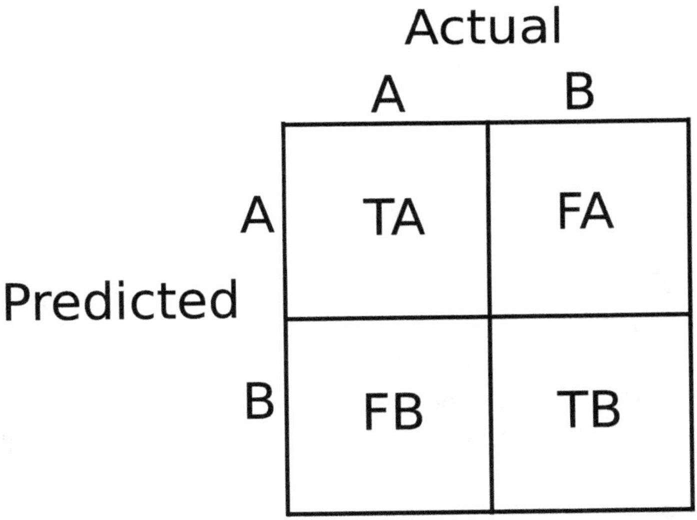

Figure 4.1: Confusion matrix for binary classifier.

In a perfect classifier FP and FN will be zero. A classifier can also be perfect in a negative sense where the opposite of what it says is always correct. In this case TP and TN will be zero. The fraction of correct classifications is called the accuracy of the classifier. It is defined as

$$Accuracy = \frac{TP + TN}{TP + TN + FP + FN}$$

The accuracy is not the only way to measure the performance of a classifier. We can also define a true positive and a false positive rate as follows:

$$TPR = \frac{TP}{TP + FN}$$

$$FPR = \frac{FP}{FP + TN}$$

TPR is the probability that if there is an actual positive then the classifier will correctly indicate positive. FPR is the probability that if there is an actual negative then the classifier will incorrectly indicate positive. You can also define a true negative and false negative rate.

$$TNR = 1 - TPR$$

$$FNR = 1 - FPR$$

The nice thing about TPR and FPR is that they are not sensitive to the proportion of actual positives and negatives. They give a more stable indication of the classifier's performance. In some applications they are more informative than just the overall accuracy of the classifier. For example in medical testing if a person has the disease then you want to maximize the probability of detecting it, i.e. you want to maximize TPR. At the same time if the person does not have the disease you want to minimize the probability of falsely saying that they do.

A ROC curve is just a plot of TPR versus FPR. If the classifier only outputs a positive or negative response then TPR and FPR are fixed values and the plot consists of just a single point. If the classifier outputs the probability of a positive response then the values of TPR and FPR will depend on where we set the threshold of what is considered a positive or negative response. As the threshold is varied from 1 to 0, the values of TPR and FPR will both start at 0 and end at 1. A plot of these values is what is known as an ROC curve. Figure 4.2 shows the ROC curve for SPY being classified by TLT. Details for creating this plot will be described in section 4.2.

When the threshold is greater than 1 the classifier will have no positive responses so both TPR and FPR will be zero. As the threshold drops below 1 positive responses start to appear and if the classifier is any good they should mostly be correct. If the classifier is perfect then TPR will continue to climb until it reaches 1 with FPR staying at 0. As the threshold is lowered

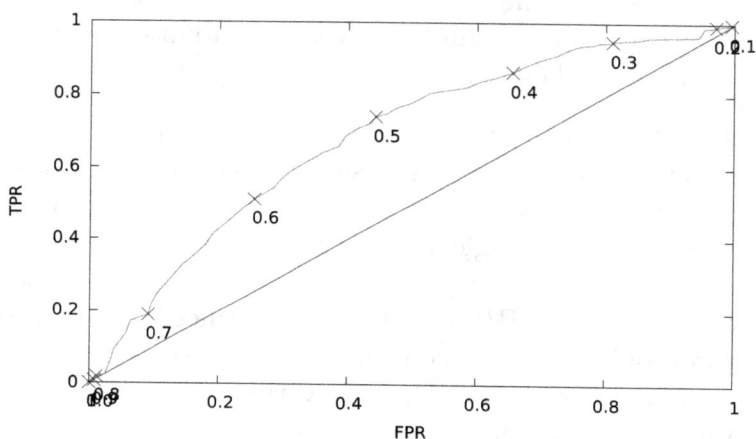

Figure 4.2: ROC curve for SPY being classified by TLT. Labeled points are for predicted probabilities of 0.1, 0.2, 0.3,...,0.9, 1.0. Note the endpoints of 0.1, 0.2 and 0.8, 0.9, 1.0 are crowded on the corners. The straight line $(TPR = FPR)$ is the 'no better than chance' boundary. Everything above is better.

to zero the classifier outputs nothing but positive responses so that FN and TN are both zero and TPR and FPR are both equal to 1. The ROC curve always ends at the point (1,1).

If a classifier has little or no predictive power then the ROC curve will be near to the $TPR = FPR$ line. To see this, just look at the expected number of the four possible outcomes of classification when the classification probabilities are independent of the actual probabilities. The closer the ROC curve gets to the point (0,1) and the larger the area between the ROC curve and the $TPR = FPR$ line, the better the classifier overall.

The ROC curve can help you consider the trade off between benefits and costs of true positives and false positives, or for that matter true negatives and false negatives.

4.2 Classifying SPY with each of the other ETFs individually

Now we will quantify the ability to classify SPY using each of the other 11 ETFs by using the program class2kde.

Classifying SPY with TLT we run class2kde like this:

```
./class2kde tltoc.dat resp_spy.dat h.dat 1388 1
```

where `tltoc.dat` is the training file consisting of daily open-to-close data on TLT as fractional differences, and `resp_spy.dat` is the class file consisting of a single column of 1's and 0's indicating whether SPY went up or down for each day. The training and class files were discussed previously in chapter 2. The number 1388 specifies the number of records (lines) in the training and class files, and the number 1 specifies the number of columns in the training file.

File `h.dat` contains 2 floating point (decimal) numbers per line, separated by a space, for each column in the training file. In this case we only have 1 column in the training file, so there is only 1 line of 2 numbers, separated by a space, where the 1st number is determined by the variance and number of points of the 0 response data file `tltoc_r0.dat`, and the 2nd number is determined by the variance and number of points of the 1 response data file `tltoc_r1.dat`. These response files were discussed in chapter 3.

The formula for the h values is [1]

$$h = \sigma \left(\frac{4}{3n} \right)^{\frac{1}{5}} \tag{4.1}$$

where n is the number of points (lines), and σ is the variance of the numbers in each file. For `tltoc_r0.dat` the number of points is 659, and $\sigma = 0.007350803125830$ giving an h value of 0.002125912843750. For `tltoc_r1.dat` the number of points is 729, and $\sigma = 0.007116455934767$ giving an h value of 0.002017000501517. So the `h.dat` file consists of a single line with the numbers: 0.002125912843750 0.002017000501517

The h values for the other ETFs calculated from their corresponding 0 response and 1 response files, over the period Jan 3, 2007 to July 5, 2012, are shown in table 4.1.

Going back to the command line shown at the beginning of this section:

```
./class2kde tltoc.dat resp_spy.dat h.dat 1388 1
> class2kde.out
```

Here we are saving the output of class2kde to the file `class2kde.out`, since the output normally goes to the

---

[1]Applied Smoothing Techniques for Data Analysis, Bowman & Azzalini, 1997

ETF	h for 0 response	h for 1 response
TLT	0.002125912843750	0.002017000501517
IEF	0.001018399591997	0.001007294361221
SHY	0.000259954420830	0.000259599593323
QQQ	0.003220899652066	0.002779076237679
XLF	0.005705425814207	0.005864604739372
LQD	0.001814455035685	0.001643831535581
GLD	0.003090325535082	0.002667920311950
USO	0.005151871035609	0.004847457040999
EWZ	0.005621447608302	0.004628150600282
FXC	0.001385874317186	0.001185771124713
FXE	0.001279874488968	0.001122348091930

Table 4.1: h values for the 0 response and 1 response of predictor ETFs based on equation 4.1 for the data plotted in figures 3.1 through 3.11.

screen (stdout). The output file contains 1388 lines of numbers which look like this:

```
0.6133463858 0
0.4178740406 1
0.6184530686 0
. . . . . . . . . . . . .
0.3693067421 1
0.6836276315 1
0.4194296597 0
```

Each line consists of a predicted probability (floating point number between 0 and 1), followed by a space, then a 0 or 1 (1 for up, 0 for down or unchanged) indicating whether SPY went up or down for that day.

This output file we will process in 2 ways. First we'll produce an ROC curve for gnuplot with an awk script, then we'll use another awk script to produce statistics based on a desired threshold probability.

4.2.1 ROC curves for the other ETFs individually classifying SPY

To produce the ROC plot of figure 4.2 we sort the output of class2kde, then run the awk script class2kde2roc.awk [2] on the sorted output like this:

```
sort -b -n -k 1,1n class2kde.out | tac > class2kde.sort
awk -f class2kde2roc.awk class2kde.sort > class2kde.roc
```

The sorting is done based on the numeric value of the first column (predicted probability) of class2kde.out, in descending order (starting with 1.0 and going to 0.0). The above sort command runs on the Linux command line. For Windows, you could use either the native MS-DOS sort or *Cygwin* sort. Mac OS X also has a sort. Note that piping the results of sort to tac simply reverses the order of the results. Linux sort does have a '-r' option for reversing the order of results but it doesn't seem to work in this situation. Saving the results of sorting to file class2kde.sort, we run the awk script class2kde2roc.awk on it. The output of this awk script is stored in file class2kde.roc, and this can be plotted in gnuplot, as shown in figure 4.2, like this:

```
gnuplot> unset key
gnuplot> set xlabel "FPR"
gnuplot> set ylabel "TPR"
gnuplot> plot 'class2kde.roc' using 1:2 with lines,
  '' using 1:2:($4==1 ? 1 : 1/0) with points lc rgb 'blue',
  x, '' using 1:2:($4==1 ? sprintf("%1.1f",column(3)) : 1/0)
  with labels offset 1.0,-1.0
```

where the 4 lines of the above plot command must all be on one line.

---

[2]See our *data mining and machine learning page* for this and all other awk scripts mentioned in this book.

Figures 4.3 through 4.12 show ROC curves for each of the other 10 ETFs (IEF, SHY, QQQ, XLF, LQD, GLD, USO, EWZ, FXC, FXE) individually classifying SPY.

The ROC curves for TLT, IEF, and SHY are all fairly similar. The curves for QQQ and XLF are comparatively fantastic. They rise steeply from the origin and don't turn significantly toward the right until after a probability threshold of 0.7. LQD and GLD are the worst, staying close to the $TPR = FPR$ line. The ROC curve for USO is fair, being similar to SHY. EWZ is good, being only a little worse than QQQ and XLF. FXC and FXE are similar to TLT, IEF, and SHY.

These ROC curves give us a good idea of how well any of the 11 other ETFs can individually classify SPY.

4.2.2   Statistics for the other ETFs individually classifying SPY

The second way we will process the output of class2kde is with the awk script `class2kde.awk`. This script reads the unsorted output of class2kde, as well as a threshold probability value, and outputs statistics on 2 lines. The output statistics is based on the calculation of the 4 values: TP, FP, FN, and TN, defined in section 4.1. The first line of output contains the 4 integers: TP, FP, FN, and TN. The second line

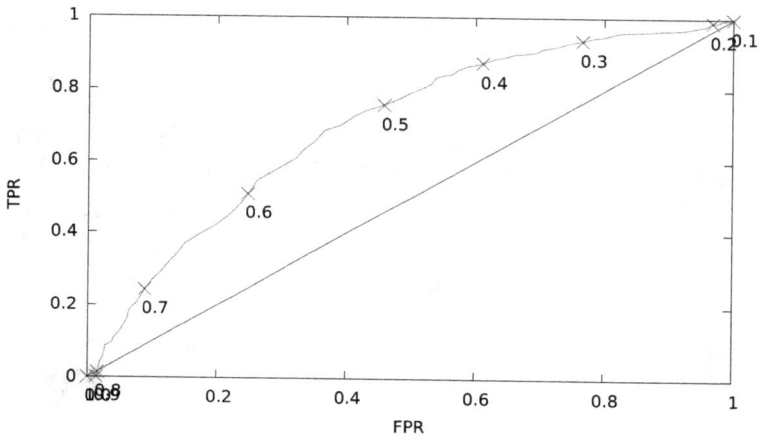

Figure 4.3: ROC curve for SPY being classified by IEF. Labeled points are for predicted probabilities of 0.1, 0.2, 0.3,...,0.9, 1.0. Note the endpoints of 0.1, 0.2 and 0.8, 0.9, 1.0 are crowded on the corners. The straight line $(TPR = FPR)$ is the 'no better than chance' boundary. Everything above is better.

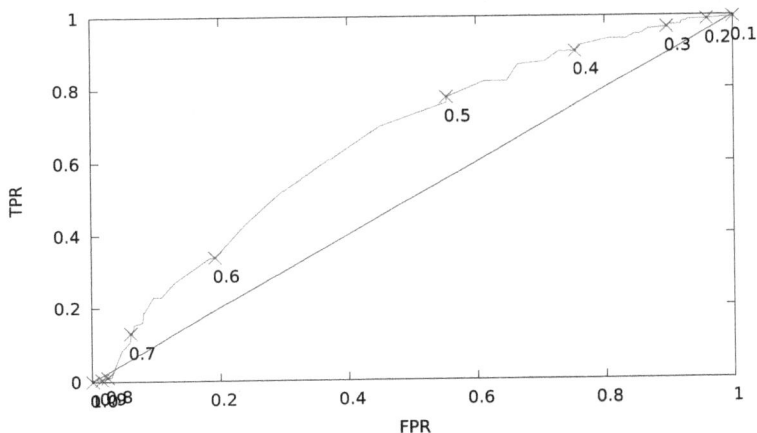

Figure 4.4: ROC curve for SPY being classified by SHY. Labeled points are for predicted probabilities of 0.1, 0.2, 0.3,...,0.9, 1.0. Note the endpoints of 0.1, 0.2 and 0.8, 0.9, 1.0 are crowded on the corners. The straight line $(TPR = FPR)$ is the 'no better than chance' boundary. Everything above is better.

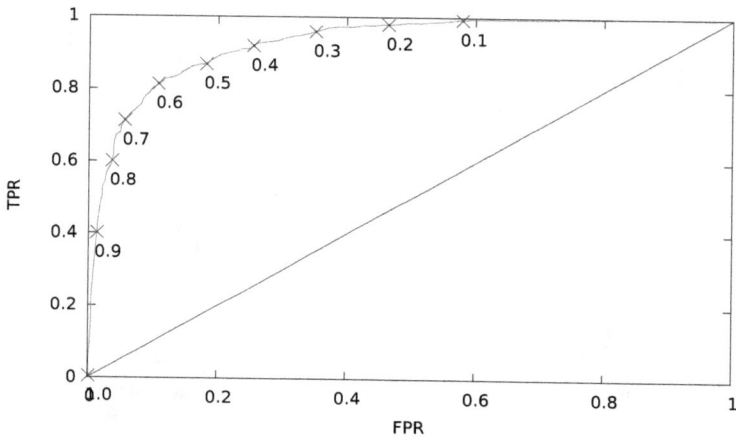

Figure 4.5: ROC curve for SPY being classified by QQQ. Labeled points are for predicted probabilities of 0.1, 0.2, 0.3,…,0.9, 1.0. Note the endpoints of 0.1, 0.2 and 0.8, 0.9, 1.0 are crowded on the corners. The straight line ($TPR = FPR$) is the 'no better than chance' boundary. Everything above is better.

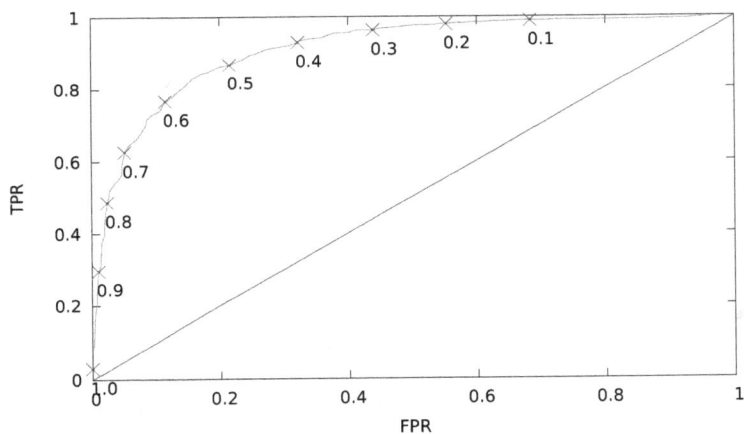

Figure 4.6: ROC curve for SPY being classified by XLF. Labeled points are for predicted probabilities of 0.1, 0.2, 0.3,...,0.9, 1.0. Note the endpoints of 0.1, 0.2 and 0.8, 0.9, 1.0 are crowded on the corners. The straight line $(TPR = FPR)$ is the 'no better than chance' boundary. Everything above is better.

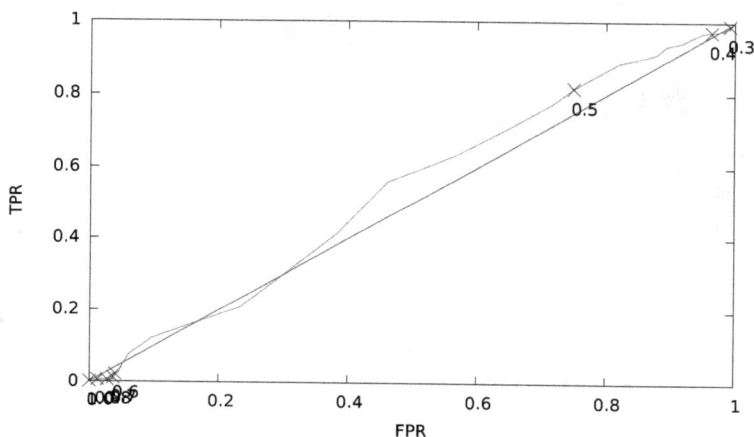

Figure 4.7: ROC curve for SPY being classified by LQD. Labeled points are for predicted probabilities of 0.1, 0.2, 0.3,...,0.9, 1.0. Note the endpoints of 0.1, 0.2 and 0.8, 0.9, 1.0 are crowded on the corners. The straight line ($TPR = FPR$) is the 'no better than chance' boundary. Everything above is better.

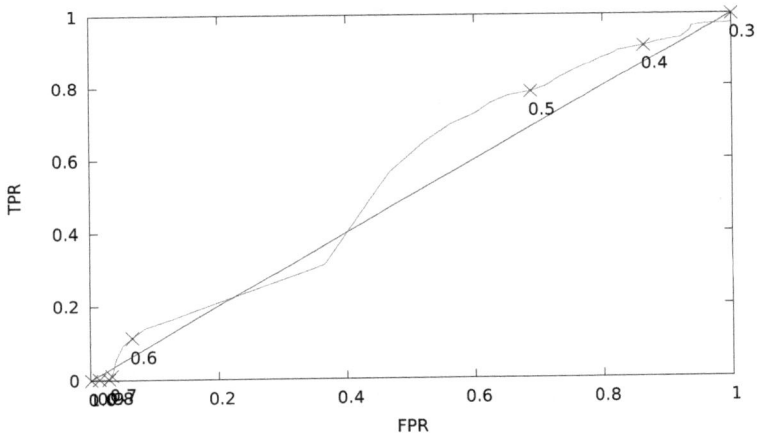

Figure 4.8: ROC curve for SPY being classified by GLD. Labeled points are for predicted probabilities of 0.1, 0.2, 0.3,...,0.9, 1.0. Note the endpoints of 0.1, 0.2 and 0.8, 0.9, 1.0 are crowded on the corners. The straight line $(TPR = FPR)$ is the 'no better than chance' boundary. Everything above is better.

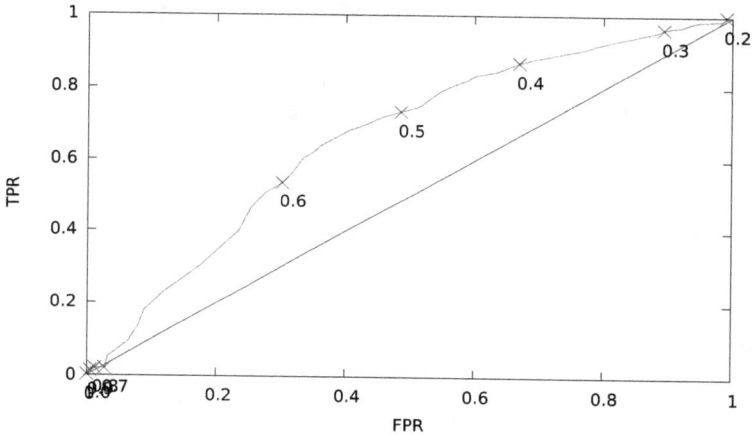

Figure 4.9: ROC curve for SPY being classified by USO. Labeled points are for predicted probabilities of 0.1, 0.2, 0.3,...,0.9, 1.0. Note the endpoints of 0.1, 0.2 and 0.8, 0.9, 1.0 are crowded on the corners. The straight line $(TPR = FPR)$ is the 'no better than chance' boundary. Everything above is better.

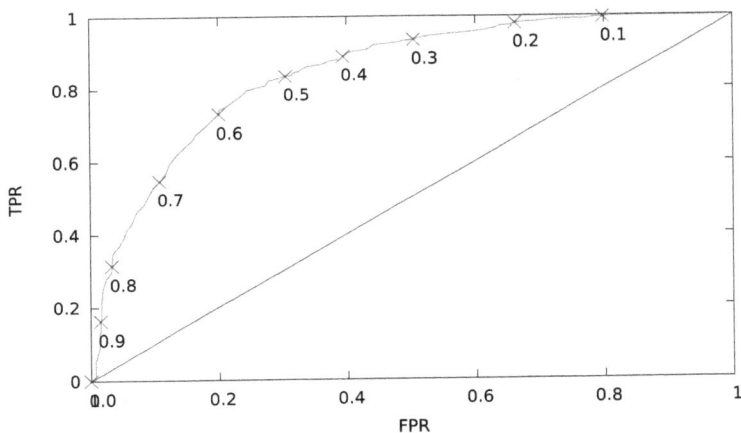

Figure 4.10: ROC curve for SPY being classified by
EWZ. Labeled points are for predicted probabilities of
0.1, 0.2, 0.3,...,0.9, 1.0. Note the endpoints of 0.1,
0.2 and 0.8, 0.9, 1.0 are crowded on the corners. The
straight line $(TPR = FPR)$ is the 'no better than
chance' boundary. Everything above is better.

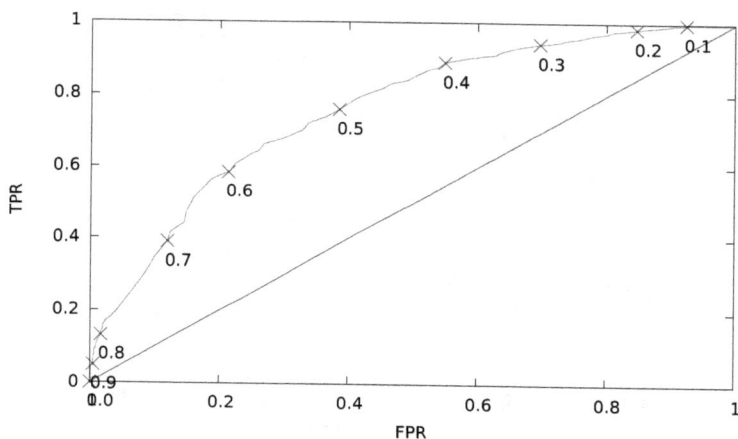

Figure 4.11: ROC curve for SPY being classified by FXC. Labeled points are for predicted probabilities of 0.1, 0.2, 0.3,...,0.9, 1.0. Note the endpoints of 0.1, 0.2 and 0.8, 0.9, 1.0 are crowded on the corners. The straight line $(TPR = FPR)$ is the 'no better than chance' boundary. Everything above is better.

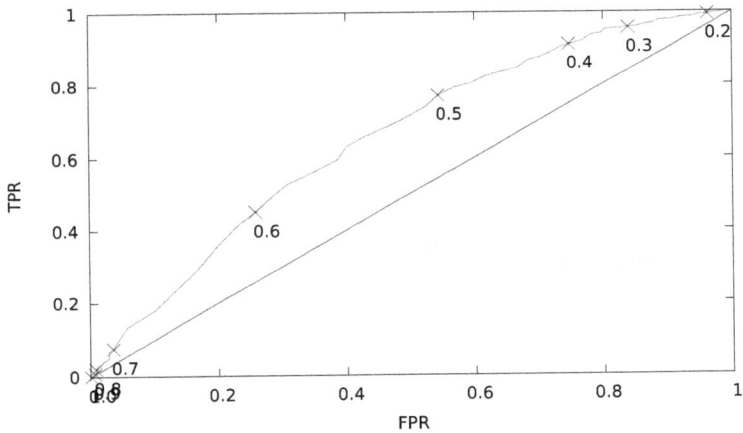

Figure 4.12: ROC curve for SPY being classified by FXE. Labeled points are for predicted probabilities of 0.1, 0.2, 0.3,...,0.9, 1.0. Note the endpoints of 0.1, 0.2 and 0.8, 0.9, 1.0 are crowded on the corners. The straight line $(TPR = FPR)$ is the 'no better than chance' boundary. Everything above is better.

contains 3 floating point numbers:

- True positive rate or sensitivity
  $TPR = TP/(TP + FN)$ = probability of predicting P given that actual is P.

- False positive rate or sensitivity
  $FPR = FP/(FP + TN)$ = probability of predicting P given that actual is N.

- $Accuracy = (TP + TN)/(TP + TN + FP + FN)$

For example, to run `class2kde.awk` on the output of class2kde generated earlier, with a threshold probability of 0.5, we enter the command line:

```
awk -f class2kde.awk -v thr=0.5 class2kde.out
```

whose output are the 2 lines:

```
540 292 189 367
0.74074 0.44310 0.65346
```

which tells us that $TP = 540$, $FP = 292$, $FN = 189$, $TN = 367$, $TPR = 0.74074$, $FPR = 0.44310$, and $Accuracy = 0.65346$.

For trading purposes, a good metric to use from these results is the ratio TPR/FPR. If the classification

is worth anything this ratio should be larger than 1.
The larger this number, the better. In this case it's
$0.74074/0.44310 = 1.67172$.

If we re-run `class2kde.awk` as above, with threshold
probabilities ranging from 0.1 to 0.9 in intervals of 0.1,
the largest value of TPR/FPR is 2.07908 at a threshold probability of 0.7.

If, for each of the other 10 predictor tickers, we run
class2kde, then feed its output to `class2kde.awk`, as
we just did with the results for TLT, the highest ratio of
TPR/FPR at intervals of 0.1 for each ticker is shown
in table 4.2.

4.3 Classifying SPY with pairs of the other ETFs

Now we'll pair up the 11 ETFs we've chosen as prediction candidates to see if we can get better results.

For data file preparation, the class file remains unchanged. The training file has one more column added
to it corresponding to the fractional change in open-
to-close of the other ETF, and the h file has one more
line added to it corresponding to the h values of the 0
response and the 1 response of the other ETF.

Running class2kde on all possible pairs of the 11 other

Rank	ETF	Probability	TPR / FPR
1	QQQ	0.9	29.32284
2	XLF	0.9	27.90019
3	FXC	0.9	10.85275
4	EWZ	0.9	10.67040
5	IEF	0.7	2.77434
6	USO	0.7	2.26154
7	SHY	0.7	2.14695
8	TLT	0.7	2.07908
9	FXE	0.7	2.07166
10	LQD	0.7	1.81188
11	GLD	0.9	1.80263

Table 4.2: Highest ratio of TPR/FPR for each ticker as gotten from class2kde.awk for threshold probabilities ranging from 0.1 to 0.9 in intervals of 0.1. Sorted by TPR/FPR.

ETFs, we get 55 results (11 choose $2 = 55$) [3].

The highest ratio of TPR/FPR for the top 30 pairs of the 11 predictor tickers is shown in table 4.3.

ROC curves for the top 5 pairs of table 4.3 are shown in figures 4.13 through 4.17.

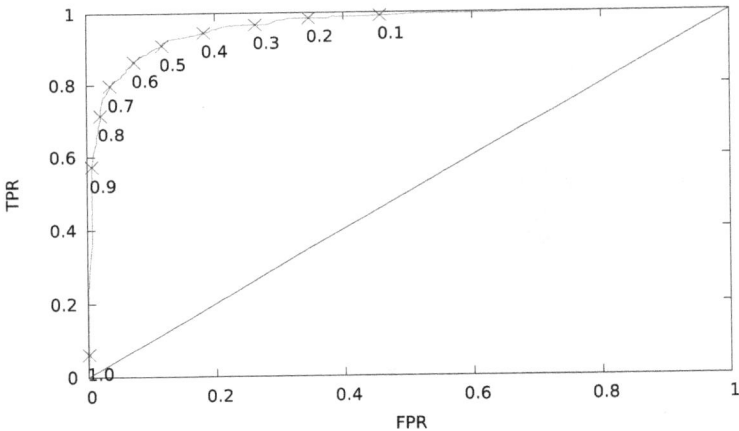

Figure 4.13: ROC curve for SPY being classified by the top ranked pair QQQ-XLF. Labeled points are for predicted probabilities of 0.1, 0.2, 0.3,...,0.9, 1.0. The straight line ($TPR = FPR$) is the 'no better than chance' boundary. Everything above is better.

Note that the top 11 pairs in table 4.3 have TPR/FPR ratios better than the top ranked single ETF of table

---

[3]n choose $k = \binom{n}{k} = \frac{n!}{(n-k)!k!}$ = number of ways to choose k items from a set of n.

Rank	ETF	Probability	TPR / FPR
1	QQQ-XLF	0.9	75.54545
2	XLF-FXC	0.9	45.07143
3	QQQ-USO	0.9	39.52448
4	QQQ-FXE	0.9	39.00847
5	SHY-QQQ	0.9	38.74953
6	QQQ-GLD	0.9	37.58757
7	QQQ-EWZ	0.9	37.28748
8	IEF-QQQ	0.9	34.80231
9	XLF-EWZ	0.9	32.31631
10	TLT-QQQ	0.9	31.23060
11	XLF-LQD	0.9	29.70810
12	QQQ-FXC	0.9	29.11668
13	QQQ-LQD	0.9	28.30323
14	IEF-XLF	0.9	27.57084
15	XLF-FXE	0.9	27.34432
16	TLT-XLF	0.9	24.70351
17	XLF-GLD	0.8	21.99868
18	XLF-USO	0.9	19.31456
19	SHY-XLF	0.9	16.84901
20	SHY-FXC	0.9	15.67692
21	USO-FXE	0.9	14.44079
22	EWZ-FXC	0.9	13.65392
23	IEF-FXC	0.9	12.47036
24	GLD-EWZ	0.9	11.95022
25	LQD-EWZ	0.9	11.84575
26	TLT-EWZ	0.9	11.67106
27	IEF-EWZ	0.9	11.52554
28	USO-EWZ	0.9	11.21292
29	USO-FXC	0.9	10.62109
30	SHY-EWZ	0.9	9.71719

Table 4.3: Highest ratio of TPR/FPR for the top 30 pairs of 11 predictor tickers (there are 55 pairs) as gotten from class2kde.awk for threshold probabilities ranging from 0.1 to 0.9 in intervals of 0.1.

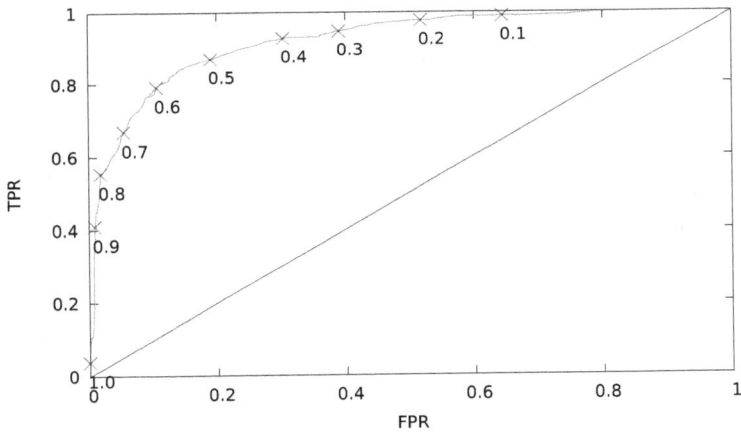

Figure 4.14: ROC curve for SPY being classified by the 2nd ranked pair XLF-FXC. Labeled points are for predicted probabilities of 0.1, 0.2, 0.3,. . .,0.9, 1.0. The straight line $(TPR = FPR)$ is the 'no better than chance' boundary. Everything above is better.

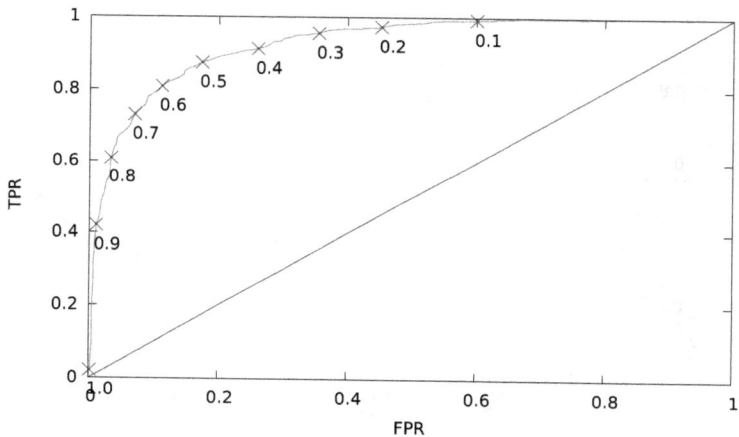

Figure 4.15: ROC curve for SPY being classified by the 3rd ranked pair QQQ-USO. Labeled points are for predicted probabilities of 0.1, 0.2, 0.3,...,0.9, 1.0. The straight line $(TPR = FPR)$ is the 'no better than chance' boundary. Everything above is better.

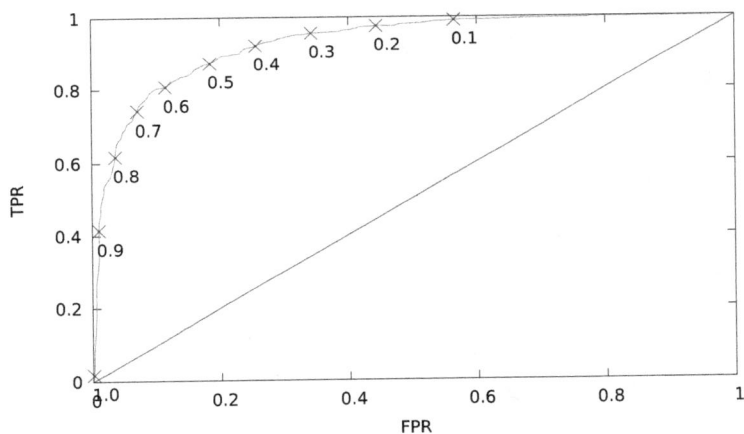

Figure 4.16: ROC curve for SPY being classified by the 4th ranked pair QQQ-FXE. Labeled points are for predicted probabilities of 0.1, 0.2, 0.3,...,0.9, 1.0. The straight line $(TPR = FPR)$ is the 'no better than chance' boundary. Everything above is better.

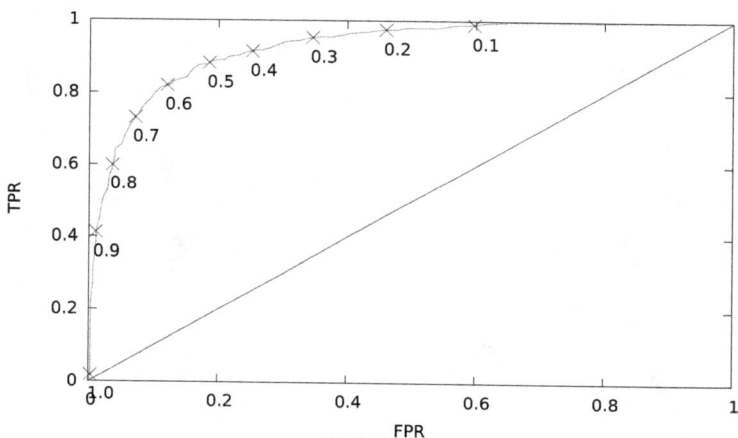

Figure 4.17: ROC curve for SPY being classified by the 5th ranked pair SHY-QQQ. Labeled points are for predicted probabilities of 0.1, 0.2, 0.3,...,0.9, 1.0. The straight line $(TPR = FPR)$ is the 'no better than chance' boundary. Everything above is better.

4.2. The steepness of the ROC curves for the top 5 pairs also show this. So we definitely benefit from using pairs of ETFs as opposed to singles.

4.4 Classifying SPY with 3 of the other ETFs

Now moving from pairs to triples to see if results improve. There are 11 choose 3 = 165 triples.

The top 30 of the highest TPR/FPR ratio for each ticker triple is shown in table 4.4.

With pairs, the top two TPR/FPR ratios were about 75 and 45, whereas with triples the highest is 64, while the top 7 are larger than 45. So the highest ratio drops, but we get an overall improvement of best performers.

ROC curves for the top 5 triples of table 4.4 are shown in figures 4.18 through 4.22.

4.5 Classifying SPY with 4 of the other ETFs

Now moving from triples to quadruples. There are 11 choose 4 = 330 quads.

Rank	ETF	Probability	TPR / FPR
1	QQQ-XLF-LQD	0.9	64.51758
2	QQQ-XLF-FXC	0.9	56.96234
3	QQQ-XLF-FXE	0.9	54.76648
4	TLT-QQQ-XLF	0.9	48.47446
5	QQQ-XLF-USO	0.9	48.24794
6	QQQ-XLF-GLD	0.9	48.13509
7	SHY-QQQ-USO	0.9	46.72967
8	QQQ-XLF-EWZ	0.9	44.28551
9	SHY-QQQ-XLF	0.9	43.18082
10	IEF-QQQ-FXC	0.9	43.01224
11	IEF-QQQ-XLF	0.9	42.77892
12	IEF-QQQ-EWZ	0.9	38.75700
13	SHY-QQQ-FXE	0.9	36.83608
14	QQQ-GLD-FXC	0.9	36.49671
15	XLF-LQD-EWZ	0.9	36.15815
16	QQQ-USO-EWZ	0.9	34.84553
17	SHY-QQQ-GLD	0.9	34.68863
18	QQQ-LQD-FXC	0.9	33.64056
19	QQQ-GLD-FXE	0.9	33.55931
20	TLT-IEF-XLF	0.9	32.54991
21	QQQ-GLD-USO	0.9	32.03441
22	QQQ-LQD-GLD	0.9	31.53221
23	QQQ-LQD-EWZ	0.9	31.10613
24	IEF-XLF-FXC	0.9	30.42753
25	XLF-GLD-FXC	0.9	29.62372
26	QQQ-LQD-USO	0.9	29.29730
27	XLF-FXC-FXE	0.9	28.92094
28	QQQ-EWZ-FXC	0.9	28.60216
29	QQQ-USO-FXE	0.9	28.21226
30	TLT-XLF-FXC	0.9	27.85102

Table 4.4: Highest ratio of TPR/FPR for the top 30 of each ticker triple of 11 tickers (there are 165 of them) as gotten from class2kde.awk for threshold probabilities ranging from 0.1 to 0.9 in intervals of 0.1.

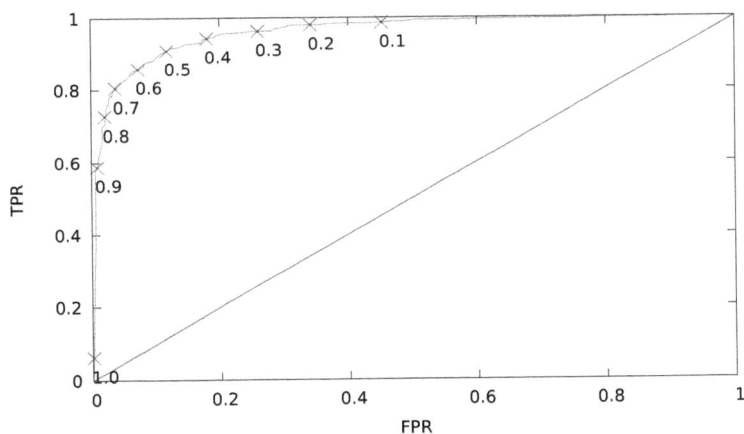

Figure 4.18: ROC curve for SPY being classified by the top ranked triple QQQ-XLF-LQD. Labeled points are for predicted probabilities of 0.1, 0.2, 0.3,...,0.9, 1.0. The straight line $(TPR = FPR)$ is the 'no better than chance' boundary. Everything above is better.

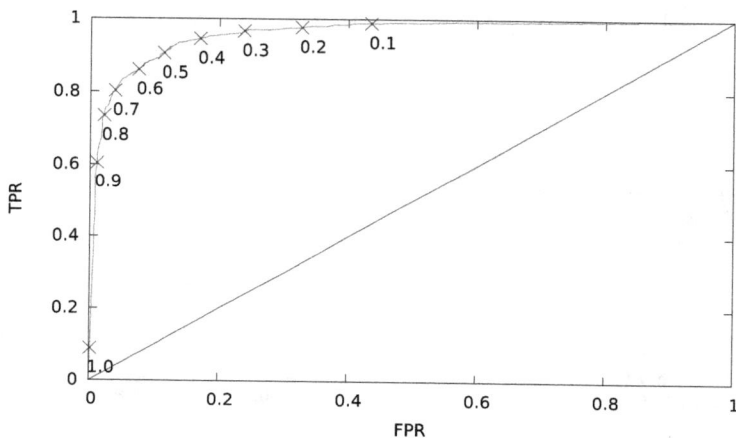

Figure 4.19: ROC curve for SPY being classified by the 2nd ranked triple QQQ-XLF-FXC. Labeled points are for predicted probabilities of 0.1, 0.2, 0.3,. . . ,0.9, 1.0. The straight line $(TPR = FPR)$ is the 'no better than chance' boundary. Everything above is better.

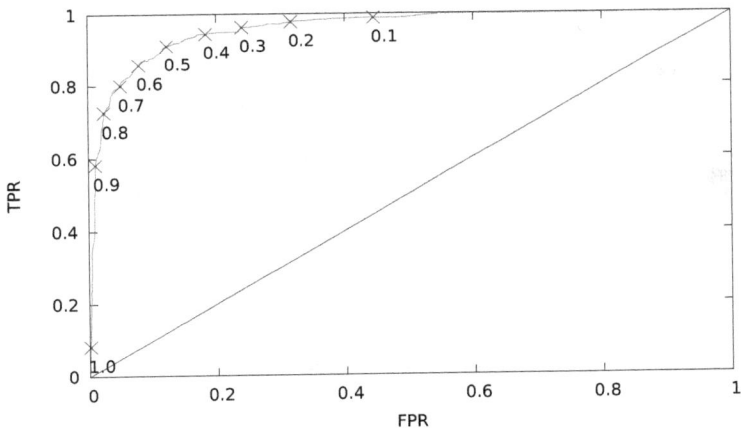

Figure 4.20: ROC curve for SPY being classified by the 3rd ranked triple QQQ-XLF-FXE. Labeled points are for predicted probabilities of 0.1, 0.2, 0.3,...,0.9, 1.0. The straight line ($TPR = FPR$) is the 'no better than chance' boundary. Everything above is better.

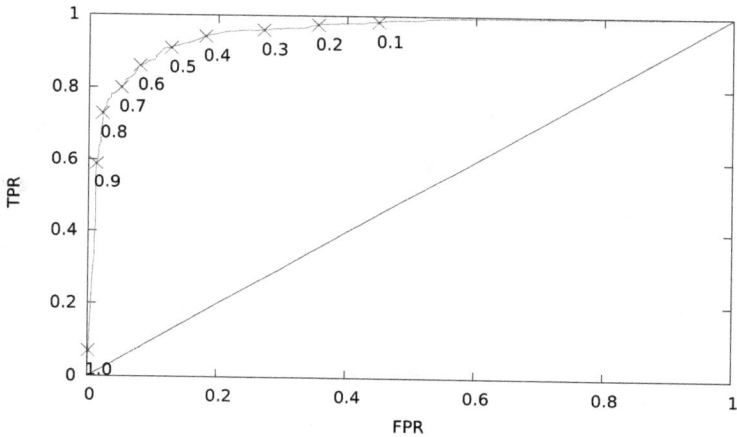

Figure 4.21: ROC curve for SPY being classified by the 4th ranked triple TLT-QQQ-XLF. Labeled points are for predicted probabilities of 0.1, 0.2, 0.3,...,0.9, 1.0. The straight line $(TPR = FPR)$ is the 'no better than chance' boundary. Everything above is better.

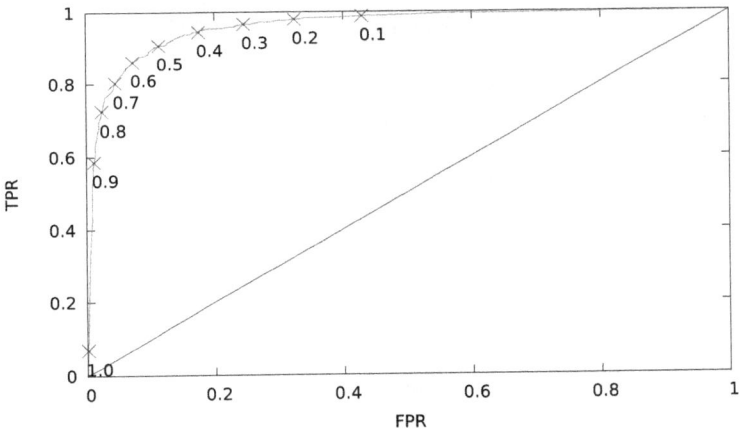

Figure 4.22: ROC curve for SPY being classified by the 5th ranked triple QQQ-XLF-USO. Labeled points are for predicted probabilities of 0.1, 0.2, 0.3,. . .,0.9, 1.0. The straight line $(TPR = FPR)$ is the 'no better than chance' boundary. Everything above is better.

The top 30 of the highest TPR/FPR ratio for each ticker quad is shown in table 4.5.

Going from triples to quads the top ranked TPR/FPR ratio drops from 64 to 57, but now the top 9 are above 45, whereas with triples the top 7 were.

ROC curves for the top 5 quads of table 4.5 are shown in figures 4.23 through 4.27.

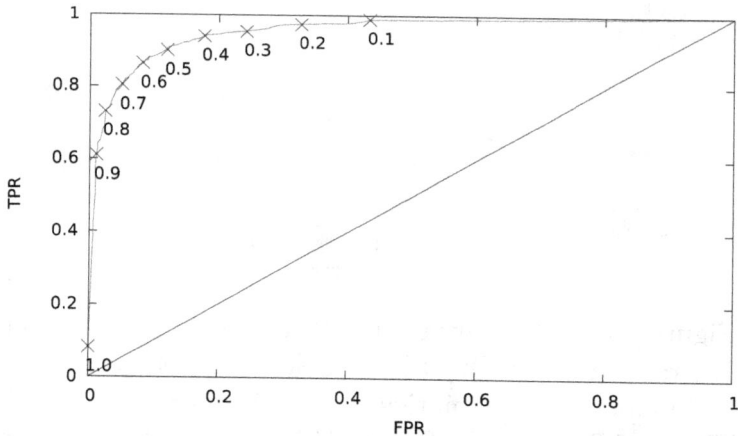

Figure 4.23: ROC curve for SPY being classified by the top ranked quadruple QQQ-XLF-GLD-USO. Labeled points are for predicted probabilities of 0.1, 0.2, 0.3,...,0.9, 1.0. The straight line $(TPR = FPR)$ is the 'no better than chance' boundary. Everything above is better.

Rank	ETF	Prob	TPR / FPR
1	QQQ-XLF-GLD-USO	0.9	57.47928
2	SHY-QQQ-XLF-LQD	0.9	57.09134
3	QQQ-XLF-LQD-GLD	0.9	56.44539
4	TLT-QQQ-XLF-LQD	0.9	55.54143
5	QQQ-XLF-LQD-FXC	0.9	51.75124
6	QQQ-XLF-FXC-FXE	0.9	50.84679
7	QQQ-XLF-GLD-FXC	0.9	50.73394
8	TLT-QQQ-XLF-GLD	0.9	49.94316
9	IEF-QQQ-XLF-LQD	0.9	49.03954
10	SHY-QQQ-XLF-FXE	0.9	44.78770
11	TLT-QQQ-XLF-USO	0.9	44.38580
12	IEF-QQQ-XLF-GLD	0.9	43.98389
13	QQQ-XLF-LQD-EWZ	0.9	41.50494
14	QQQ-XLF-USO-FXC	0.9	40.32960
15	QQQ-XLF-LQD-FXE	0.9	40.23929
16	SHY-QQQ-XLF-USO	0.9	39.78708
17	QQQ-XLF-USO-FXE	0.9	39.51549
18	QQQ-LQD-GLD-FXC	0.9	39.43493
19	QQQ-XLF-LQD-USO	0.9	39.06328
20	QQQ-XLF-USO-EWZ	0.9	37.64290
21	QQQ-XLF-EWZ-FXC	0.9	37.47813
22	QQQ-XLF-GLD-FXE	0.9	36.32774
23	TLT-QQQ-XLF-FXC	0.9	36.24566
24	QQQ-XLF-GLD-EWZ	0.9	34.04887
25	SHY-QQQ-XLF-GLD	0.9	33.74739
26	IEF-QQQ-XLF-FXC	0.9	33.74739
27	TLT-QQQ-XLF-FXE	0.9	32.99396
28	TLT-SHY-QQQ-XLF	0.9	32.39154
29	TLT-IEF-QQQ-XLF	0.9	32.24108
30	TLT-QQQ-XLF-EWZ	0.9	31.49518

Table 4.5: Highest ratio of TPR/FPR for the top 30 of each ticker quadruple of 11 tickers (there are 330 of them) as gotten from class2kde.awk for threshold probabilities ranging from 0.1 to 0.9 in intervals of 0.1.

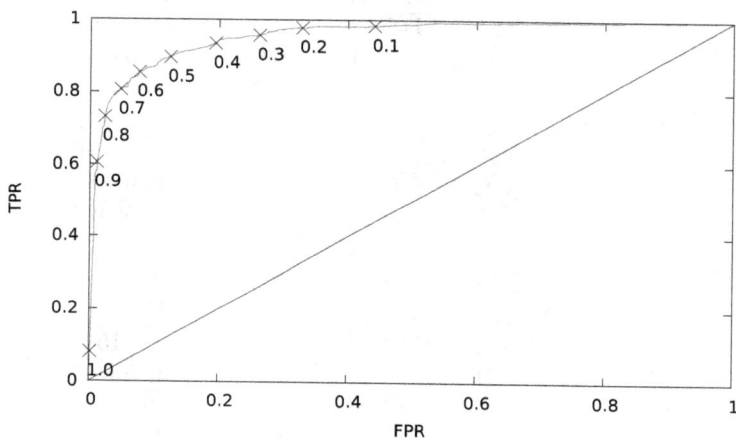

Figure 4.24: ROC curve for SPY being classified by the 2nd ranked quadruple SHY-QQQ-XLF-LQD. Labeled points are for predicted probabilities of 0.1, 0.2, 0.3,...,0.9, 1.0. The straight line ($TPR = FPR$) is the 'no better than chance' boundary. Everything above is better.

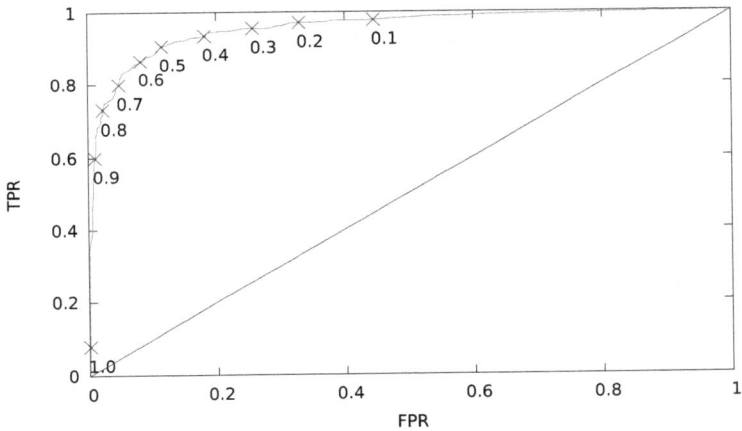

Figure 4.25: ROC curve for SPY being classified by the 3rd ranked quadruple QQQ-XLF-LQD-GLD. Labeled points are for predicted probabilities of 0.1, 0.2, 0.3,...,0.9, 1.0. The straight line ($TPR = FPR$) is the 'no better than chance' boundary. Everything above is better.

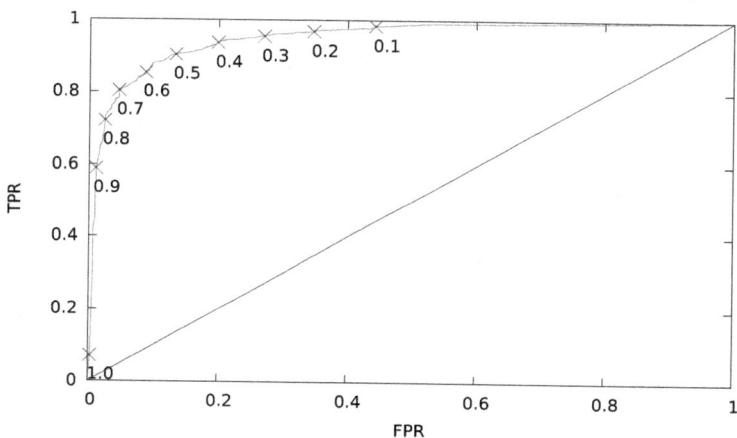

Figure 4.26: ROC curve for SPY being classified by the 4th ranked quadruple TLT-QQQ-XLF-LQD. Labeled points are for predicted probabilities of 0.1, 0.2, 0.3,...,0.9, 1.0. The straight line $(TPR = FPR)$ is the 'no better than chance' boundary. Everything above is better.

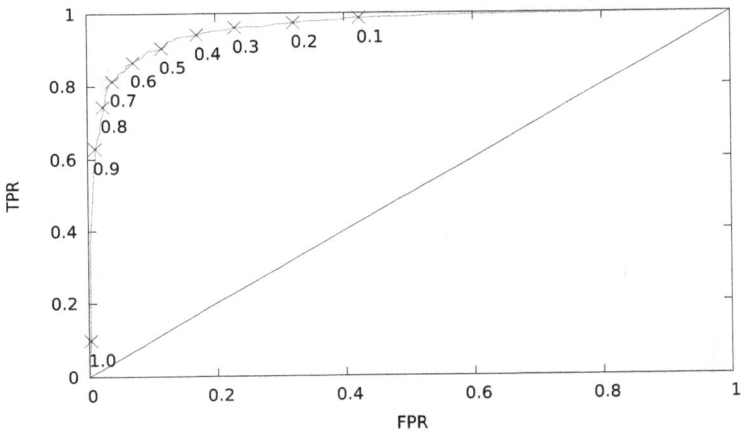

Figure 4.27: ROC curve for SPY being classified by the 5th ranked quadruple QQQ-XLF-LQD-FXC. Labeled points are for predicted probabilities of 0.1, 0.2, 0.3,...,0.9, 1.0. The straight line $(TPR = FPR)$ is the 'no better than chance' boundary. Everything above is better.

4.6 Summary of results

Table 4.6 combines the top 5 results of tables 4.2 through 4.5.

Group size	Rank	ETF	Prob	TPR / FPR
1	1	QQQ	0.9	29.32284
	2	XLF	0.9	27.90019
	3	FXC	0.9	10.85275
	4	EWZ	0.9	10.67040
	5	IEF	0.7	2.77434
2	1	QQQ-XLF	0.9	75.54545
	2	XLF-FXC	0.9	45.07143
	3	QQQ-USO	0.9	39.52448
	4	QQQ-FXE	0.9	39.00847
	5	SHY-QQQ	0.9	38.74953
3	1	QQQ-XLF-LQD	0.9	64.51758
	2	QQQ-XLF-FXC	0.9	56.96234
	3	QQQ-XLF-FXE	0.9	54.76648
	4	TLT-QQQ-XLF	0.9	48.47446
	5	QQQ-XLF-USO	0.9	48.24794
4	1	QQQ-XLF-GLD-USO	0.9	57.47928
	2	SHY-QQQ-XLF-LQD	0.9	57.09134
	3	QQQ-XLF-LQD-GLD	0.9	56.44539
	4	TLT-QQQ-XLF-LQD	0.9	55.54143
	5	QQQ-XLF-LQD-FXC	0.9	51.75124

Table 4.6: Combining the top 5 results of tables 4.2 through 4.5. Top 5 of highest TPR/FPR ratio for group sizes 1 through 4.

Looking at table 4.6, we see that for single tickers, the

top ranked TPR/FPR ratio was 29. For groups of 2 tickers, the top ranked ratio jumped up to 75. For triples it fell down to 64, then for quadruples it fell again to 57.

Why did the top ranked ratio sharply increase going from group size 1 to 2? Notice the top ranked group of size 2 is QQQ-XLF. These 2 tickers happen to be the top 2 performers of group size 1. So the answer seems to be when you combine the 2 best performers, you get even better results.

Why did the top ranked ratio decrease going from group size 2 to 3? The top performer of group size 3 is QQQ-XLF-LQD. The 1st 2 members of this group happen to be the best performer of group size 2. But the 3rd member, is no where to be found in the top 5 of group size 2. It looks like the answer may be when you combine the 2 best performers with a bad performer, you get worse results than using only the 2 best.

Why did the top ranked ratio decrease yet again going from group size 3 to 4? The top performer of group size 4 is QQQ-XLF-GLD-USO. Its first two members are the top ranked of group size 2 which has a higher score. But the 3rd member, GLD, isn't to be found anywhere in the top 5 of the smaller groups. The 4th member, USO, is in the top 5 of group sizes 2 and 3, but it belongs to groups that have lower scores. So it appears that combining the 2 best performers with a good performer and a bad performer results in a slightly worse performance.

If we look at the overall change in the TPR/FPR ratio with successively larger groups, we see a steady improvement. For example, the 11th best ratio with single tickers is 1.8, with double tickers the 11th best is 29.7, with triples it's 42.7, and with quads it's 44.3. This rise in the average score might be useful in strategies that use a form of buy signal averaging.

Note that every one of the top 5 for every group size in table 4.6 has a threshold probability of 0.9, except for one (the 5th ranked of group size 1 has 0.7). These points are very near to the TPR (vertical) axis on the ROC curves. This suggests that the 'natural' choice of 0.5 for threshold probability can often be a bad one, at least with stock or ETF data.

5

Using the Results for Trading

Once you've identified that a set of attributes may be useful in classifying an object, then you can try to use the attributes to predict the class of an object. So for example, we discovered above that QQQ and XLF together are extremely good predictors of whether SPY closes up or down. Knowing this, we can now use the price of QQQ and XLF during the trading day to calculate a corresponding probability of SPY ending the day up or down. If SPY is currently down, but QQQ and XLF indicate a high probability of SPY closing the day up, then you buy SPY, and vice versa.

To do this, we need a slightly different tool than the

class2kde program that we used above. Now we want to do a classification prediction for an object whose class we don't know. The C program xclass2kde [1] is the tool to use for this. Like class2kde it takes a training file and a corresponding class file but it also takes an additional file of unclassified records. So for the example above, the training file would consist of records of the returns on QQQ and XLF, the class file would be the corresponding classification of the return on SPY, and the extra file would contain the current returns on QQQ and XLF that are used to classify what the return on SPY will be.

You can run xclass2kde periodically throughout the trading day with the current returns on QQQ and XLF and use the prediction to trade SPY. The prediction should usually agree with what SPY is currently doing in which case you do nothing, but the possibility for profit arises when the prediction does not agree with the current situation. Also, the prediction will probably be most accurate in the last half of the trading day, but things can change all the way up to closing. This is where the advantage of a probability comes in. You can bet according to how high or how low the probability is. One method to use is the Kelly system as described in our book *Bet Smart: The Kelly System for Gambling and Investing*.

---

[1]xclass2kde can be downloaded from our *data mining and machine learning web page*.

Let's run the example of using QQQ and XLF to classify SPY with xclass2kde. The time period for the class and training data will be what we've been using: January 3, 2007 to July 5, 2012 (1,388 records). The class file will be the same binary open-to-close file for SPY that we've been using. The training file will be the open-to-close fractional difference data from QQQ and XLF over the given period, that is the same data we've been using. And the unclassified record file will cover the 23 trading days from July 6, 2012 to August 7, 2012.

The h file, generated as described in section 4.2 is hqqqxlf.dat consisting of the 2 lines:

```
0.003220899652066  0.002779076237679
0.005705425814207  0.005864604739372
```

Running xclass2kde like this:

```
./xclass2kde qqqxlf_oc.dat resp_spy.dat
 hqqqxlf.dat qqqxlf_oc2.dat 1388 2
```

we get the following results:

```
0.204581985119732
0.511186232272524
0.002900645747666
0.488545140253164
```

```
0.396531997235939
0.998804642717405
0.406422625958776
0.416719085332928
0.954584137221950
0.559316016237670
0.016868350868550
0.969228210145457
0.045495726209921
0.528669826781132
0.453640633073067
0.995828753965757
0.352371254211871
0.374900753405834
0.031537215098047
0.784894431835953
0.859888773002915
0.612855904427995
0.784638310878173
```

which are 23 probabilities.

Now to check how well we did, we generate a binary open-to-close file for SPY over the given 23 trading days (resp_spy2.dat), then compare it to the prediction based on a given threshold probability. This is done with the awk script xclass2kde.awk like this:

```
awk -f xclass2kde.awk -v thr=0.5 xclass2kde.out
  resp_spy2.dat
```

The output is:

```
0 1 0 0 0 1 0 0 1 1 0 1 0 1 0 1 0 0 0 1 1 1 1
8 3 5 7
0.61538 0.30000 0.65217
```

The 1st line of output is the prediction based on the given threshold probability. In this case there are 23 1's and 0's. The 2nd line is 4 integers: TP (true positives), FP (false positives), FN (false negatives), and TN (true negatives). The 3rd line is 3 floating point numbers: TPR (probability of predicting P given that actual is P), FPR (probability of predicting P given that actual is N), and Accuracy = (TP+TN)/(TP+TN+FP+FN).

So out of a total of 23 predictions, TP = 8, FP = 3, FN = 5, TN = 7, TPR = 0.61538, FPR = 0.30000, and Accuracy = 15/23 = 0.65217.

Running xclass2kde.awk as above for threshold probabilities from 0.1 to 0.9 in increments of 0.1, we show the statistics results in table 5.1.

Looking at table 5.1, because of the small number of records (23), we see that FPR is 0.0 at threshold probabilities of 0.7, 0.8, and 0.9, so that the ratio TPR/FPR is ∞ in those three cases. Since a good threshold probability to use is one that maximizes this ratio, we would choose from these 3, and since the highest accuracy among those 3 is 73.9%, we would choose 0.7 as the threshold probability. The row corresponding to a threshold probability of 0.7 shows that the total number of correct predictions is $TP+TN = 7+10 = 17$ out

Prob	TP	FP	FN	TN	TPR	FPR	Accur
0.1	13	6	0	4	1.00000	0.60000	0.73913
0.2	13	6	0	4	1.00000	0.60000	0.73913
0.3	12	6	1	4	0.92308	0.60000	0.69565
0.4	10	5	3	5	0.76923	0.50000	0.65217
0.5	8	3	5	7	0.61538	0.30000	0.65217
0.6	7	1	6	9	0.53846	0.10000	0.69565
0.7	7	0	6	10	0.53846	0.00000	0.73913
0.8	5	0	8	10	0.38462	0.00000	0.65217
0.9	4	0	9	10	0.30769	0.00000	0.60870

Table 5.1: Running xclass2kde for classifying SPY over 23 trading days from July 6, 2012 to August 7, 2012, and making predictions based on a given threshold probability (0.1, 0.2,...,0.8, 0.9).

of a total of 23 predictions. The probability of a coin toss with a fair coin achieving this is $\binom{23}{17}/2^{23} = 0.012$ or 1.2%.

Table 5.2 shows the binary representation of what actually happened in the 1st column, and the remaining columns show the prediction based on the given threshold probability.

In our example in this book, we used the open-to-close returns. There is nothing special about this time period. You can use other time periods, shorter or longer. But shorter time periods may prove more profitable since there are more opportunities for trading and the process can be turned into a dynamic one with inputs

Actual	Threshold Probability								
	0.1	0.2	0.3	0.4	0.5	0.6	0.7	0.8	0.9
1	1	1	0	0	0	0	0	0	0
0	1	1	1	1	1	0	0	0	0
0	0	0	0	0	0	0	0	0	0
0	1	1	1	1	0	0	0	0	0
1	1	1	1	0	0	0	0	0	0
1	1	1	1	1	1	1	1	1	1
0	1	1	1	1	0	0	0	0	0
1	1	1	1	1	0	0	0	0	0
1	1	1	1	1	1	1	1	1	1
1	1	1	1	1	1	0	0	0	0
0	0	0	0	0	0	0	0	0	0
1	1	1	1	1	1	1	1	1	1
0	0	0	0	0	0	0	0	0	0
0	1	1	1	1	1	0	0	0	0
1	1	1	1	1	0	0	0	0	0
1	1	1	1	1	1	1	1	1	1
1	1	1	1	0	0	0	0	0	0
0	1	1	1	0	0	0	0	0	0
0	0	0	0	0	0	0	0	0	0
1	1	1	1	1	1	1	1	0	0
1	1	1	1	1	1	1	1	1	0
0	1	1	1	1	1	1	0	0	0
1	1	1	1	1	1	1	1	0	0

Table 5.2: Comparing the binary representation of what actually happened over 23 trading days (July 6, 2012 to August 7, 2012), to the xclass2kde prediction based on a given threshold probability.

frequently updated and the prediction being automatically checked against the current situation.

Instead of a current-time prediction, one can also use the software discussed in this book to predict a time period entirely, or disjointly, in the future. In this case it's no longer like pairs trading. For instance, in our example of classifying SPY, we used the open-to-close of other ETFs to determine what SPY will do over the same period. But we could also have used the open-to-close of the previous day, or the close-to-open to determine what SPY will do on the open-to-close today. Generally the cost of doing this is an overall reduction in ability to classify. Relationships usually dissipate as the time to prediction increases.

6

Conclusions

- The Bayesian analysis performed by programs
  class2kde and xclass2kde in this book will exploit almost any kind of relationship that may
  exist between stocks or ETFs.

- The program class2kde helps us determine how
  useful some given historical data is for classifying (predicting up or down). More data can be
  better, but not necessarily.

- Plotting conditional probability density functions
  of the training data, split by response, using kernel density estimation, helps to visually determine predictive power (classification effectiveness).

- ROC curves are a visual aid to decide on threshold probability. They are useful with any prediction system whose output is a probability.

- TPR and FPR are not sensitive to the proportion of actual positives and negatives. The *Accuracy* is sensitive, and can be misleading.

- TPR/FPR ratios are good numerical indicators for deciding on a threshold probability.

- Once we've used class2kde to identify the best attributes for prediction, and have used the ROC curve and TPR / FPR ratios to choose the best threshold probability, we can use xclass2kde to predict an object whose class we don't know.

- With xclass2kde we got a 73.9% accuracy in predicting SPY over the last 23 trading days using data from the previous 5 1/2 years. The probability of a coin toss with a fair coin achieving this is 1.2%.